Traditions Around The World

Costumes

by Danielle Sensier

Thomson Learning

New York

Traditions Around The World

Books in this series:

Costumes

Masks

Cover: Traditional garment of the Rajasthan region in Northwest India.

Consultant: Anthony Shelton, Keeper of Non-Western Art and Anthropology, Royal Pavillion Art Gallery and Museums, Brighton, England.

First published in the
United States in 1995 by
Thomson Learning
115 Fifth Avenue
New York, NY 10003

First published in Great Britain in 1994 by
Wayland (Publishers) Ltd.

Library of Congress Cataloging-in-Publication Data
Sensier, Danielle.
  Costumes / by Danielle Sensier.
     p.   cm.—(Traditions around the world)
  Includes bibliographical references (p.   ) and index.
  ISBN 1-56847-227-7
  1. Costume—Juvenile literature. [1. Costume] I. Title.
II. Series
GT518.S45   1994
391—dc20   94-20747

Printed in Italy

Picture acknowledgments:

The publishers wish to thank the following for providing the photographs for this book: Bryan & Cherry Alexander 15; Bruce Coleman Limited 14-15, 16-17 (Erwin & Peggy Bauer), 18 (Charles Henneghien), 34-35 (Gerald Cubitt); Sue Cunningham Photographic 12, 20-21, 25; Robert Estall 28-29 (Angela Fisher & Carol Beckwith), 30-31 (Carol Beckwith); Eye Ubiquitous *cover* (David Cumming), 10 (G.R. Richardson), 16 (L. Fordyce), 27 (Tony Brown), 35 (top) (David Cumming), 36 (top) (Paul Thompson), 36 (bottom) (P.M. Field), 38-39 (David Cumming), 44-45 (Matthew McKee); Jimmy Holmes 6, 6-7, 7; Life File 8-9 (Emma Lee), 24-25 (Juliet Highet), 37 (Paul Fisher), 39 (Hiroshi Isobe); Link 13 (Orde Eliason), 26-27 (Eric Meacher), 35 (bottom) (Shari Kessler), 41 and 42-43 (Orde Eliason); Photri 14, 16, 18 (top); South American Pictures 21, 22 and 22-23 (Tony Morrison); Still Pictures 30-31 (Mark Edwards); Tony Stone Worldwide 8 (Ken Welsh), 12-13 (David Hanson); Tropix 28 (D. Davis), 42 (D. Charlwood); Wayland Picture Library 11, 45.

The artwork is by Peter Bull.

Contents

Costumes around the world

NORTH AMERICA

SOUTH AMERICA

EUROPE

ASIA

AFRICA

THE PACIFIC

Introduction

Would you call your clothing traditional costume? You might be wearing modern clothes, but the style, material, or pattern of them may come from a costume that is hundreds of years old. It could even come from a country thousands of miles away.

Traditional clothing or costume is a type of dress that is worn by people who share the same nationality, religion, or customs, and it may remain the same for many centuries.

We can look at traditional clothes and costumes and discover all sorts of interesting information about the history and beliefs of the people who wear them. A thousand ancient stories are woven into the fabric of the costumes of people around the world. As well as giving us clues about the wearer's beliefs and customs, traditional dress can also tell us something about the climate that people live in, the kinds of materials they are able to use, and even the type of work they do.

These women from ▲ western China are dressed up for a wedding. Their headdresses are traditional, but some of the women also wear modern coats, with western-style buttons and lapels.

◀ The clothes of these Rajasthani women in Pushkar, India, are embroidered with gold and silver thread. The stitches are often made using a traditional tool called an *ari*, instead of a needle.

6

Traditional costumes are often made in special ways, using methods that have been passed down from generation to generation. The ways in which clothes are sewn, woven, and printed can be unique to a particular people. Designs and patterns of clothes often have special meanings. In Central Asia, a tulip motif is popular on some garments. In certain parts of this region, the tulip is the first flower to appear in the spring. It is a symbol of the happiness and new life that spring brings each year, so it is used decoratively to brighten clothing.

The colors of clothes can also tell us something about the people who wear them. In the Middle East, some clothes are decorated with blue beads or buttons. The wearer believes these will give protection against evil.

Certain costumes are worn for ceremonies such as weddings or funerals, and again the clothes can have special meanings. In many western countries, people wear black clothes when a relative or loved one has died. The black is a symbol and reminder of their sorrow over the person's death.

In some parts of the world, the clothes people wear every day are very traditional. They are the same style and use the same materials and designs as the clothing worn many years ago. However, in many places special costumes are worn only on certain occasions. The clothes that people wear every day only hint at past traditions.

By using traditional designs, patterns, and materials, we can add old meaning to modern clothes. By wearing traditional clothes or dressing up in costumes on special occasions, we are keeping some of the stories and customs of the past alive today.

▲ **Traditional clothes are made from all kinds of natural materials, including plant fibers. These sandals are made by hand from braided grass.**

Europe

▲ These Polish street musicians are wearing folk costumes. The style and color of the men's trousers and the flower designs on the woman's costume are traditional.

◀ Spanish flamenco dancers wear exciting costumes to match their lively dance routines. It is usual for the dresses to have fancy, colorful sleeves, and for women to wear real or silk flowers in their hair.

In Europe there are many different kinds of traditional clothes and costumes. Most are connected with the country or area in which people live. Although few traditional costumes are now worn every day, people still wear them on special occasions or to do certain jobs.

Wearing a traditional costume gives people a sense of belonging to a certain group. Throughout history, a great many Europeans have left their original countries to live elsewhere, sometimes where the culture and traditions have been very different from their own. In some cases, people's way of life has changed a great deal. Wearing traditional costumes has helped these people to remember – and has let other people know about – their homeland and culture.

In some countries in Eastern Europe, such as Poland, people are keeping alive the traditions of folk music, dance, and art that began in small farming communities many years ago. These people wear beautiful costumes to dance to folk music during festivals, or on special occasions such as weddings. At wedding ceremonies in the town of Kraków, the bridegroom wears a special headdress covered with motifs of flowers and peacocks. These are symbols of good luck.

Traditional costumes are still worn for many kinds of dances. In Spain, flamenco dancers wear special costumes. Flamenco dancing is very graceful and exciting to watch. It can be seen at many festivals. The women wear brightly colored dresses with lots of frills and flounces, and the men wear tight-fitting trousers and bolero jackets. Spanish gypsies, called *gitanos*, are thought to be the best flamenco dancers. The style of the flamenco costume originally came from the gypsies.

▲ This herdsman from Lapland in northern Scandinavia wears the traditional red and blue colors of the Saami costume. Thick layers of clothing and a fur hat keep him warm in the cold climate.

Nomadic peoples often place great importance on traditional dress. Because they do not live in one place all of the time, they identify with the group and its traditions by wearing traditional costume. In this way, they keep some of their past history alive.

The Saami people of Scandinavia were originally nomadic. They herded reindeer, moving from place to place to find good grazing ground for the animals. Today, some Saami still herd reindeer, and they wear traditional Saami clothing of warm woolen capes and special scarves and hats. Other Saami now live in different countries, often hundreds of miles away from one another. They still share the same customs and language. To keep their traditions alive, they cross countries to get together for special reunions; on these occasions they wear elaborate costumes in traditional colors.

Sometimes the materials used to make clothes are part of a tradition. In Scotland, the kilt is a kind of skirt worn by men for Highland dancing and on special occasions. Scottish army regiments also wear kilts as part of their ceremonial uniforms. Each kilt has a plaid pattern called a tartan. There are lots of different tartans, each one belonging to a different Scottish clan. The tartan identifies the clan to which a Scottish person's family originally belonged.

While certain costumes can be the traditional dress of a country, some people wear traditional clothes to show that they see themselves as a group that is different from the other people in a country. In Brittany, a region of northwest France, some of the people do not want to be ruled by the French government. They would like to be independent. At local festivals such as the fishermen's fête at Concarneau, the Bretons wear traditional costume to show that they feel different from the people living in the rest of France. The women wear dresses with white cotton aprons and tall bonnets made of stiff white linen, decorated with embroidery or lace. The men wear boleros and breeches and black, roll-brimmed hats.

◀ **A man wearing a Scottish kilt.**

Using costume to express feelings of pride for a place is also popular in independent European countries that were once ruled by another country. Latvia used to be part of the former USSR. Now it is independent, and the Latvians are bringing back some of their old traditions. There is an old Latvian proverb that says "what is red is beautiful," so traditional costumes are often decorated with red embroidery. The national costume for Latvian women includes a wide-sleeved blouse and full skirt, a long, fringed headscarf, and special sandals called *pastali*.

People who have special jobs or who belong to a particular group can sometimes be identified by their traditional uniforms. In Greece, the guardsmen outside the parliament building are easily recognizable because of their unusual skirts, stockings, and shoes.

In Mediterranean ▶ countries, such as Italy and Portugal, many older women continue to wear black clothes long after the funeral of a relative – and sometimes for the rest of their lives.

Main picture: The uniform of these Greek guardsmen is a sign of their special status, which sets them apart from other people. The skirts are part of an ancient Greek costume, no longer worn by Greek civilians.

12

▲ This man lives in England, but his family comes from India. His turban shows that he follows the Indian Sikh religion.

In many European countries people are studying traditional costumes in order to understand more about how people lived in the past. Although modern clothing in Europe looks very similar in each country, many of the styles and fabrics have traditional origins. Capital cities in Europe such as Paris, Rome, and London are famous fashion centers of the world, where designers create new clothes and new styles. Yet the clothes are not always as modern as they look because the ideas that designers use are often taken from traditional costumes.

Today there are many groups of people who have gone to live in Europe from other parts of the world. The costumes that they take with them help them to remember their customs and are adapted to make the clothes and costumes in Europe more rich and varied.

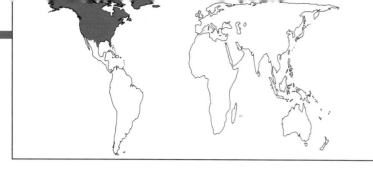

North America

The people in the United States and Canada are from many different countries and cultures, so there are hundreds of different types of traditional dress. A lot of these clothes come from people who brought their traditions with them from Europe. Other main types of traditional clothing come from Native American peoples, who have lived in these lands for thousands of years.

Long before the European settlers arrived in the sixteenth century, Native Americans of the Great Plains hunted buffalo for clothing and food. The skins of the buffalo were scraped clean and then tanned and dried, and the hooves were boiled down and used to make varnish for the hides. These were made into large robes, with colorful scenes from daily life or stories of great warriors painted on them with natural dyes.

Some of the descendants of these original peoples have kept old traditions going – they make handicrafts and clothes using ancient methods. Keeping these traditions alive is important because some are connected with the Native Americans' religious beliefs and stories that are thousands of years old.

▲ A traditional Navajo blanket is woven on a loom made from tree trunks. Many textiles and crafts made in traditional ways are now sold to tourists, providing an important source of income.

◀ This costume, worn by a chief of the Stoney people of Canada, includes a special harness for his horse. Notice the traditional use of feathers, beaded fringes, and bold, geometric patterns.

The Navajo people from the southwest United States are very skilled weavers. They believe that a traditionally woven blanket becomes a part of nature. Navajo blankets were originally woven on looms made out of tree trunks. These were held in place by rocks. As they were woven, the blankets appeared to grow out of the earth. This is similar to their story of the origin of their people. The Navajo believe that their people once lived beneath the earth and grew out of the ground. According to the story, the first person to teach the Navajo to weave was one of these ancestors, called Spider Woman.

These brightly colored "eye-dazzler" blankets are still part of Navajo traditional costume. Originally, the wool used to make the blankets was dyed using a mixture of berries, roots, and minerals. Red dye was difficult to produce, but a solution came when the European settlers arrived. Blankets belonging to Europeans contained red wool, and the Navajo unraveled this and used it for their own new costumes.

The encounter between the first European settlers and Native Americans also influenced the clothing of the settlers. Native Americans in the northwest United States and Canada wore leggings and moccasins made from the furs and skins of deer, beavers, and foxes. The settlers started to use these materials to make warm clothes, such as beaver-skin hats.

In the far north of Canada and in parts of Alaska, near the Arctic, the Inuit peoples have traditional clothing that reflects the cold conditions in which they live. Today they wear waterproof clothing, made of modern materials thousands of miles away, but on long hunting expeditions some Inuit wear traditional clothes because they are considered to be warmer.

Traditional Inuit clothes are made from the skins and furs of animals – such as seals, polar bears, caribou, and Arctic foxes – found in the area in which they live. The clothing has a double layer of animal skin. The inner layer is worn with the fur facing in and the outer layer with the fur facing out. The Inuit were the inventors of a coat called the parka, which has been adapted into a style of warm jacket in other parts of the world. The traditional parka is made of seal skin and has a fur-lined hood, which makes it warm, waterproof, and lightweight.

The everyday work clothing of early European settlers in North America created many new types of clothes that are now considered to be traditional. The workclothes of cowboys in the West were durable and practical. They wore cotton or wool shirts, strong leather boots, and blue denim jeans reinforced with copper rivets. Denim jeans are now worn all over the world. Hats like those worn by the original cowboys are still worn today in some of the southern states of the United States, especially in Texas. They are called Stetsons, after a hat maker from Philadelphia named John B. Stetson. He began to mass-produce this type of hat in Philadelphia in 1865.

A Canadian Mountie. ▶

Some traditional outfits have been used to create a strong national symbol. In Canada, the traditional uniform of the Canadian Mounted Police, who are known as Mounties, is very famous. The original Mounties were notably brave law enforcers in the backwoods of Canada. They wore bright-red uniforms and distinctive hats. In the nineteenth century, pictures of Mounties were used to try to attract new settlers to Canada. Although the role of the Mounties is very different today, they are a symbol of national pride for Canadians.

Many North Americans whose ancestors came from Europe have traditional European national or local costumes that they wear for special festivals. The Amish people of Pennsylvania are descended from a group of Protestant Christians who migrated from Germany and Switzerland in the late 1600s. They wear very traditional clothes because of their religious customs. They reject modern manufactured things such as cars and telephones, and they believe that it is important to be humble in front of God. Bright, colorful clothes with fancy buttons and decorations are thought to be offensive to God. Both men and women wear plain, dark clothes and hats, fastened with simple hooks or strings.

17

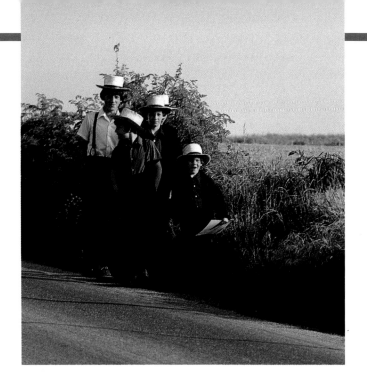

A rare photo of Amish children. Their clothing is traditionally simple and plain.

beliefs and customs. The men wear distinctive black coats and hats and do not cut the sides of their hair. When they are not wearing their hats they keep their heads covered with a small skullcap called a *kippah* or yarmulke. During some religious services, they wear small black boxes called tefillin on the forehead and left arm. These contain writings from the Jewish holy book, the Torah.

In Hasidic culture women must not be vain, so they always dress modestly and keep their heads covered. When they marry, women wear wigs in public. These traditional Jews have also settled in other places such as Jerusalem in Israel. They wear exactly the same costumes there as in New York. Like the Amish in Pennsylvania, they are following traditions for which they were once persecuted.

It is sometimes difficult to understand the religion of others. By learning about these different costumes and their history, we can gain greater understanding of one another's religious traditions.

The Amish were originally persecuted in some parts of Europe for their beliefs. They settled in America to get away from people who would not accept them. By continuing to wear their traditional clothing, they are telling people that they wish to keep their views and traditions, no matter how much the world around them changes.

In New York and other cities in North America, there is another religious group who also migrated to escape persecution. They are Hasidic Jews, whose ancestors migrated from Europe. Hasidic Jews in New York live together in a few districts and have many ancient religious

This young boy can be ▶ recognized right away as a Hasidic Jew. In keeping with his religious beliefs, the sides of his hair have not been cut and he wears a yarmulke.

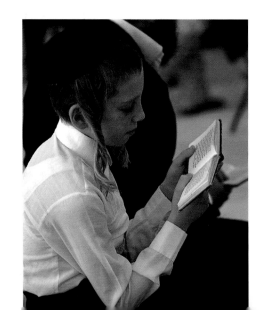

Project: Making a Native American Headband

You will need:
tapestry cloth (or canvas)
scraps of yarn (3 different colors)
large-eyed tapestry needle
scissors

1. Cut the cloth to a few inches wide. The width will vary depending on the size of the cloth holes. The suggested design needs 27 holes from top to bottom, plus a small space at either edge. Cut the cloth long enough to fit around your forehead, leaving a small space at the back of your head.

2. Work the embroidery using pieces of the yarn. Follow the suggested design by counting the colored squares – 1 square = 3 holes in the canvas.

3. Thread the needle. To make a stitch, pass the needle through one hole, working from back to front.

   Make a long straight stitch covering three holes, and pass the needle back through the canvas from front to back.

Bring the needle back diagonally to the hole next to the top of the previous stitch, and push the needle back to the front of the canvas. You are ready to make the next stitch.

4. Repeat this stitch, alternating colors according to the suggested design, until you have covered the length of the canvas. Tie any loose ends. Thread and knot a piece of yarn at each end of the canvas and tie them in a bow to secure the band around your forehead.

Central and South America

South and Central America, like North America, have a fascinating mix of traditional clothes and costumes – from clothes decorated with crushed beetles to bowler hats. Some come from European settlers, while others have origins in the dress of the original Amerindian peoples, and still more arise from a mixture of these two cultures.

The ancient civilizations of South and Central America – the Mayans, Aztecs, and Incas – valued textiles very highly. The Aztecs and Mayans even worshiped a goddess of weaving. The Aztecs would demand fine clothes and dyes from the peoples they conquered. The Incas demanded taxes from people in the form of woven cloth, costumes, and dyes. These were given to the army and to important people.

In modern Guatemala, about half of the population are descendants of the ancient Mayans. In some areas people still weave textiles on traditional back-strap looms, just as their ancestors did. Some women wear clothes today that are similar to those shown on ancient Mayan carvings.

The main part of the traditional Guatemalan costume for women is a straight, loose blouse called a *huipil,* worn with a wraparound skirt. Each village has its own *huipil* design, with distinctive colors and patterns.

Hats of many different styles are popular all over South and Central America. These felt hats are from Ecuador, and are made of llama wool. ▼

Many of the traditional ▶ clothes of Central and South America are made of wool that has been spun by hand. In the highlands of Peru, women use a simple drop-spindle – similar to a spinning top – instead of a spinning wheel. It is easy to carry and can be used anywhere.

The women wear a *tzute* on their heads. This is a piece of woven material that is worn as a loose flat turban or is used for carrying loads.

In the San Blas Islands of Panama, some Kuna women still wear traditional Amerindian costume every day. The Kuna women developed a style of appliqué that is used to make the *mola*. This is a blouse made by sewing layers of brightly colored embroidered cloth to other pieces of cloth. Each woman has several *mola* blouses, which she starts to make when she is a girl at school. New designs to be worn for a special occasion are usually made in secret, and are hidden beneath an old *mola* until the last moment. Traditional *mola* motifs include plants, animals, dreams, and scenes from everyday life,

These Kuna women are dressed up for a ▲ special occasion, so they are wearing their best clothes. Their *mola* blouses of brightly colored cloth are made with hundreds of intricate stitches.

but today's designs include modern images such as spaceships and Coca-Cola bottles.

High up in the Andean mountains of Peru and Bolivia live the Aymara people. In country areas, they still wear traditional clothes. The women wear *polleras*. These are several skirts made from brightly colored cotton, worn one on top of another. If a woman wears a number of full skirts, it is a sign of wealth. The women also wear a brightly striped cotton shawl called an *aguayo*, which is handy for carrying babies.

In the Andean mountains, people use hats to keep them warm at night and to shade them from the hot sun during the day. The Aymara men wear brightly colored knitted hats with flaps to keep their ears covered. In Bolivia, *chola* women, who are part Spanish and part Amerindian, wear bowler hats. These hats came from Great Britain, where they were very popular in the middle of the nineteenth century. Many of the British men who came to Bolivia to work on the railroads wore bowler hats, and the women adopted the style. They are now traditional wear.

◀ **These Aymara Indians in Bolivia are wearing traditional hats, shawls, and skirts. Their *pollera* skirts are also popular for dancing, since they are designed to swirl when spun.**

Wool from local animals such as llamas or alpaca has always been used in traditional Amerindian dress. When the Spanish arrived in South America, they brought merino sheep with them. The merino sheep produces a fine, silky wool. It became popular with Amerindians because it is easy to spin. In Mexico, some of the most beautiful serapes – rectangular pieces of fabric used as cloaks and blankets – and ponchos are made of tightly spun merino wool. Today most of these traditional clothes are colored using modern dyes. But Mexico is famous for one of its traditional dyes. It is a red dye called cochineal, because it is made with the dried bodies of cochineal beetles. These small insects have to be farmed on a large scale. Because it is so difficult to make, the dye is very valuable to people who want to use natural colors.

In South America and the Caribbean, there are other groups of people whose dress says something about their identity. From the sixteenth to the nineteenth century, European settlers enslaved Africans as free laborers. Some of the slaves' descendants remember the history of slavery at huge events called carnivals. Carnival celebrations first began in Christian Europe. They were held in order to have fun, break rules, and feast just before the period of Lent. Carnival became popular in the Caribbean in the eighteenth century. Just for the day, slaves were allowed to be masters, men dressed as women, and there was music and dancing, which were normally forbidden.

Traditionally, carnival costumes are used to show the struggles of people for freedom. On the Caribbean island of Trinidad, and in some parts of South America, this traditional meaning can still be seen. Many of the costumes are designed to remind people of the cruel treatment of the African slaves in the past. Other costumes are used to criticize politicians today.

Carnivals are also held in parts of North and South America such as New Orleans and Rio de Janeiro in Brazil. The costumes at these carnivals, however, rarely show the struggle of slaves for freedom. Instead, the themes of the costumes change all the time, and the designs are so fabulous that people come from around the world to watch the processions, which continue a tradition that began about 200 years ago.

◄ This carnival costume from the Caribbean symbolizes the terrible cruelty of slavery. It was not unusual for African slaves to be shackled with chains and collars.

◄ Mexican blankets, called serapes, feature distinctive bold, colorful stripes. Many are exported to other parts of the world or sold to tourists.

Africa

Africa is home to many different cultures and countries. It spans thousands of miles, and the climate and natural materials available vary greatly in different parts of the continent. Religious beliefs, politics, and trade with foreign countries have all affected traditional clothing.

Traditional African textiles are made of a wide variety of natural materials. As well as cotton and animal skins, there are some special plant fibers that can be made into cloth. Raffia is a kind of palm tree that contains a useful fiber in the stalk of its leaves. This is used for weaving traditional cloth. Another plant fiber that was used in parts of Uganda is tree bark. The bark was wrapped in banana leaves and steamed over a small fire. This made the bark turn from brown to a rich golden color. The bark was then beaten to soften it.

In the countries of West Africa, people have been producing and trading woven textiles for hundreds of years. As far back as the sixteenth century, cotton cloth from northern Nigeria was brought by camel across the huge Sahara desert to the coast, where it was shipped to countries all around the Mediterranean Sea. This trade still continues today.

▲ The Nilotic people from Kenya wear simple wraparound garments. Women decorate the beaded collars and headdresses.

In West Africa, men weave thin strips of cloth using ▶ traditional looms. They are then sown together to make large pieces of material, used for a variety of garments.

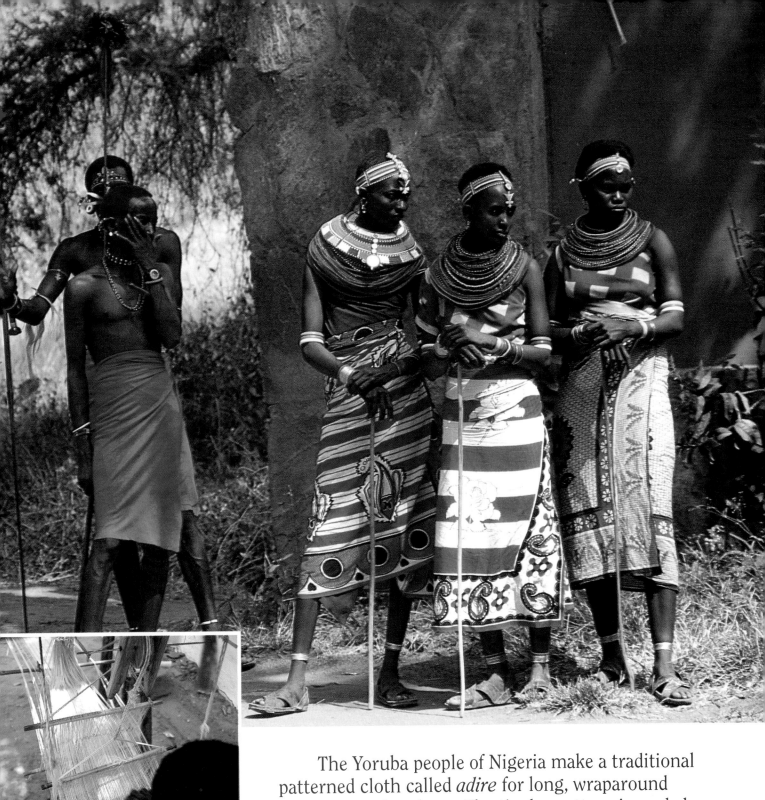

The Yoruba people of Nigeria make a traditional patterned cloth called *adire* for long, wraparound garments and turbans. The tie-dye pattern is made by tying or stitching the cloth tightly with pieces of raffia before it is dyed. The stitched or tied areas of cloth are not touched by the dye, leaving a pale pattern on a dark background. The names given to the different types of patterns include local proverbs, such as "the lazy man cannot be proud."

Throughout Africa, both men and women are involved in making traditional clothing, but they tend to do different jobs. In Morocco, spinning and weaving are thought to be women's work, while sewing, embroidery, and making tassels, braids, and fringes are all done by men. Embroidery on leather is nearly always done by men. Men also crochet and knit warm leggings and hats for themselves.

▲ These Tuareg men follow tradition by wearing veils in public. The long, loose clothing protects them against the desert heat.

The Hausa people of Nigeria wear large robes and baggy trousers. These garments are made and embroidered by men. Each stage of manufacture is carried out by a different specialist. Most designs are made up of two or more long triangular shapes called knives. Traditional patterns are known by names such as the "two knives" or the "five knives" design.

In Ghana, *kente* cloth is produced only by men, who pass on the skill to their younger brothers and to their sons when they are three or four years old. It is believed that if women took part in the weaving or sewing processes, they would be unable to have children. The cloth is made from very thin strips of fabric woven on a narrow loom and stitched together. It can then be made up into clothing. The cloth is dyed and block-printed, and the most complicated designs are saved for religious occasions.

The beliefs of a group of people are often tied up in certain traditional costumes. In some places in Africa, special clothing is worn to protect the wearer against disease, evil spirits, or enemy warriors in battle. Asante warriors once wore elaborate costumes decorated with special charms to protect them in battle.

◀ **This Beja woman from Eritrea is almost completely covered from head to toe. Although this is a modest garment, the bright colors and pattern are very attractive.**

29

In East Africa, the Masai people of Kenya value their cattle very highly. The cattle are an important source of food, fuel, and clothing, and no part of the animal is wasted. Masai women traditionally wear skirts made from strips of tanned and dried cowhide, decorated with small, brightly colored beads. The wearing of traditional cowhide skirts reflects the importance of the animal to the Masai.

The colors of costumes often have important meanings. Around the world, the meaning of certain colors can be very different. For the Chinese, red is a lucky color. However, on the island of Madagascar off the east coast of Africa, red is the color used for special burial clothes. In Ghana, red is worn for mourning. In Benin, red is worn as a symbol of warfare and power, and, farther east in Nigeria, it is a symbol of success.

Climate can determine the kind of clothes a group of people wear traditionally. The Sahara desert has a direct effect on the way the Tuareg people dress. Some are nomads – they are constantly moving with their goats and camels to find new grazing land. To keep cool in the desert heat, they wear long, loose clothes that allow the air to move around. The men wear turbans that they can wrap around their faces and mouths to protect them against the desert sands and wind. Men who keep to the old Tuareg traditions wear veils when they are with women, strangers, or their wives' relatives.

The preference for wearing long, loose clothes is also found among other nomadic peoples living in desert areas – peoples such as the Bedouin and other groups living in countries in the Middle East.

Some African costumes reveal the influence European colonists once had in certain countries. In Madagascar, the costumes of traditional male dancers are in the style of the former French colonists. They wear narrow-brimmed hats, tight trousers, long jackets, and bright cummerbunds around their waists. As people of African descent have come to live in other parts of the world, they have brought many of the bright, bold designs and styles of their traditional clothes with them. In turn, European and American-style clothing and designs are now common in many parts of Africa.

◀ **Colored beads and cowhide are used to make the traditional clothes of the Masai people of Kenya.**

Main picture: The clothes of this Hausa girl from Nigeria are decorated with beautiful embroidered motifs.

Project: Making a Tie-dye T-shirt

You will need:
old white T-shirt
wooden spoon
rubber gloves
package of cold-water dye
old plastic bowl
drying line
old newspaper
ball of string
old apron
measuring cup

1. Fold and roll the T-shirt into a long tight tube. Wind pieces of string tightly around it at regular intervals and knot the strings.

2. Put on the apron and gloves. Measure the correct amounts of water and dye, as instructed on the package, and pour them into the bowl. Mix the solution well with the spoon.

3. Place the T-shirt in the bowl of dye, making sure it is completely covered. Let it soak for the time given on the package.

4. Hang the T-shirt out to dry. If you are using an inside line, make sure you put down newspaper to catch the drips.

5. When the shirt is completely dry, remove the string and see what patterns you have made.

6. You could use a natural dye instead. Try boiling red cabbage, onion skins, or tea bags in an old saucepan. (Always ask an adult to help you with boiling water.) When the liquid has cooled down, use it in the same way as the commercial dye.

Asia

Asia is a treasure trove of beautiful traditional clothing, some of which dates back to ancient times. Silk from China has been produced and made into magnificent clothes for thousands of years. The art of traditional embroidery is so old in India that embroidery needles have been found that are 4,000 years old.

In some Asian countries, traditional costumes are very popular. A lot of importance is given to the ancient arts of needlework and other handicrafts. Girls may learn to sew from the age of six in the rural areas of Pakistan, India, and Bangladesh. One of the most elaborately decorated items a girl will work on is her wedding dress. Embroidery workshops exist in India, where men produce and sell embroidery. One of the most popular motifs of Indian embroidery is the elephant, which is a symbol of good luck.

Some of the traditional costumes in India, Pakistan, and Afghanistan include a kind of mirror-work called *shishadur*. Poor people used to decorate their clothes with shiny beetle wings, which glimmered like the jewels of the rich. Eventually, these were replaced with tiny mirrors, which are still used today. The mirrors are used to decorate all kinds of clothing, from boys' caps to brides' shawls. Even animals are draped in *shisha* costumes for certain traditional events. Some people believe that wearing these clothes will frighten away evil spirits who will be scared by seeing their own reflection in the mirrors. Flowers, parrots, and peacocks are favorite motifs for this type of traditional embroidery.

◀ In the region of Rajasthan, clothes worn on special occasions are richly embroidered with gold and silver thread. This woman's costume has also been decorated with silver disks that look like coins.

In northern Thailand and Burma each village has its own traditional clothes, which are sewn or embroidered. Tourists often buy this clothing. In other parts of Thailand some of the most beautiful traditional clothes are worn by dance groups. They are made of expensive silk in bright red, green, and gold and are decorated with gold embroidery and beads. These costumes imitate the clothes worn at the royal court in Thailand in ancient times.

Main picture: An amazing variety of fabrics, motifs, and handicrafts are used to make a traditional Indian *sari*. Some patterns have been embroidered and some have been block printed.

◀ Young girls from the hills of northern Thailand wear velvet costumes decorated with silver ornaments, tassels, and pom-poms. At the new year, wearing new clothes is thought to bring good luck.

Another way of decorating clothing is found farther south, in Indonesia. The sarong is a cool, traditional wraparound skirt that is worn by men and women in this region. Sarongs are made of fabric decorated with batik, which is an Indonesian word that means "wax writing." Hot wax is applied to the material and then the fabric is dyed. Only the areas without wax become colored. The wax pattern is applied by hand with a special kind of pen or a metal stamp.

A traditional way of making patterns on Indian clothing is block printing. This is done by dipping a carved block of wood into a color and stamping it onto the material. A pattern is made by repeating this action many times. Traditional saris are decorated in this way. The cotton sari is a length of cloth wound around the body and draped over one shoulder. It is worn by women all over India.

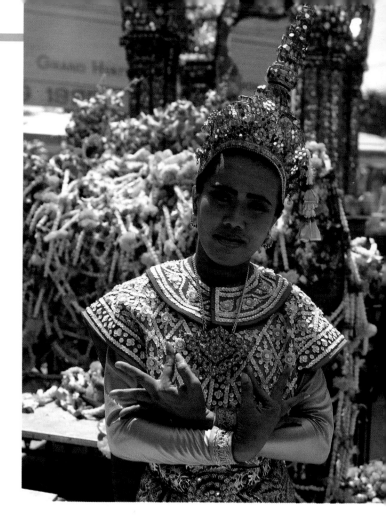

▲ This elaborate costume is worn by a temple dancer at a holy shrine in Bangkok, Thailand.

The dhoti is a cotton garment traditionally worn by men in India. It is a wide length of cotton that is wrapped around the waist, with the end pulled up between the legs and tucked in.

Cotton is used to make many of the clothes worn by people in India. Cotton grows well in the hot, moist climate, and the cloth is easy to wear because it is cool and washable. Traditionally in India, cotton was spun by hand, but during the time in which India was ruled by England, manufactured cotton was imported from other countries. The great Indian leader Mahatma Gandhi used to wear a simple dhoti to show that

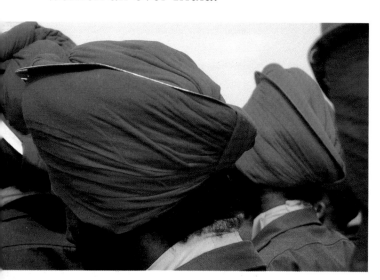

▲ These regimental turbans are worn by Indian soldiers in Calcutta. Like the man in the photograph on page 13, the soldiers are Sikhs.

he preferred traditional Indian hand-spun cotton garments to clothing that had been made from imported fabric. As a result, the wearing of traditionally spun cotton clothing became an important symbol of Indian independence. Politicians continue to encourage people to hand-spin cotton today.

In the Middle East, clothing can also be used to show a point of view. Many Palestinians are forced to live in refugee camps far away from their traditional homelands. For some of these people, wearing traditional clothing is a way of keeping their way of life alive. Palestinian women traditionally wear an ankle-length robe or coatdress, with a wide sash and a veil. The garment is decorated with cross-stitch embroidery, and at one time the color and pattern of the embroidery showed the village from which the wearer came.

Many Palestinians living in other countries prefer to wear Western styles of dress, but they often still wear a kaffiyeh, sometimes as a scarf. The kaffiyeh is a red- or black-and-white checkered traditional Arab headdress. It is also worn by people as a symbol of their Palestinian identity.

Clothing can have both political and religious meaning. Traditional Muslim women believe that the Islamic holy book, the Koran, tells them to be modest, so they wear clothes that cover their bodies almost completely. Wearing a chador, or long black gown, to hide almost all or part of their bodies is common among women who live in certain strict Muslim countries. Today, there are Muslim women around the world who used to wear Western styles of clothing, but who now wear chadors. By doing this they are showing that they prefer Islamic values to Western ideas and customs.

In north Yemen, a Muslim ▶ woman does not always cover her whole body in public. But in keeping with Muslim beliefs, her face is mostly covered by scarves as a sign of modesty.

In all parts of the world, religious groups have traditional costumes that may date back over many centuries. In Thailand, almost all young men at some time go to live in a Buddhist monastery. During this time, they stop wearing their ordinary clothing and wear a simple orange robe with no decorations. Dressing in this way helps the Buddhists to concentrate on their spiritual life instead of thinking about material things like clothes and fashion. Throughout Asia, the traditional orange robes of Buddhist monks let people know that the wearer is concentrating on his spiritual life.

In contrast to the humble robes of Buddhist monks are clothes made from Asia's most luxurious traditional material, silk. Real silk is made from the cocoon of a certain kind of caterpillar that lives in juniper trees. Silk is very warm, soft, and strong. Mongolian soldiers in ancient times used to wear it next to their skin because it is so strong that an arrowhead could not pierce it. If a soldier got shot by an arrow, the silk cloth was driven into the wound, wrapped around the arrowhead. When the arrow was pulled out of the wound, the silk would have partly protected the soldier's body, so that the wound was not too serious.

The Chinese were the first to discover this wonderful, soft thread and they guarded their secret so jealously that to take silk out of China was punishable by death. Eventually, ancient Chinese emperors became very rich by selling silk to the rest of the world.

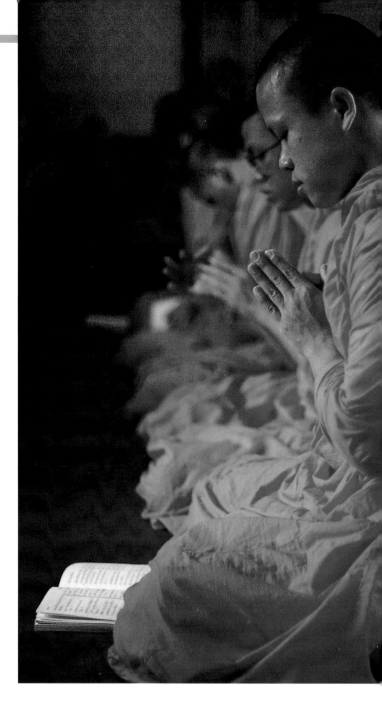

For hundreds of years, silk was a symbol of wealth in China, but during this century there was a revolution against such luxuriousness. People began to see traditional silk clothing as part of an unfair system in China, where some people were very rich and others were very poor. Traditional Chinese clothes were decorated in a way that would tell people how important a person was. A dragon decoration with

◄ These young men are learning to be Buddhist monks, and are not allowed to own wealth of any kind. Their simple orange robes are given to them by their religious followers.

This Japanese kimono is ► made of expensive silk, tied with a complicated sash. Silk is one of the world's most comfortable fabrics – but perhaps a kimono is not ideal for playing in!

five claws showed that a person was more important than someone who was only allowed to wear a dragon decoration with four claws. After 1949, there were great political changes in China, and the Chinese way of life was changed in an attempt to make people more equal. People wore a simple uniform of plain working clothes. This was supposed to show that everyone was of equal importance.

Silk is also important in Japan. A silk kimono is a traditional part of the Japanese national costume. The kimono is a loose robe wrapped over in the front and tied with a sash called an obi. The cocoons of 3,000 silkworms might be used to make one kimono. Kimonos are not usually worn every day, except by some older women. For weddings, women who choose to wear traditional dress will have a special kimono. They are often decorated with cranes, because this bird is an important symbol of happiness to Japanese people.

Although the Chinese lost their power as the only producers of silk, it is still mainly made in Asia. Now people from all around the world can enjoy wearing this traditional material.

Project: Making a Paisley Bandanna

You will need:
large plain white handkerchief
fabric crayons
tracing paper
pencil
scissors
iron

These *buta* motifs were first printed on seventeenth-century Kashmir shawls, exported by the East India Company. They became so popular that soon European factories were copying them. The pattern became known as "paisley" after the Scottish town of Paisley, which produced thousands of copies throughout the nineteenth century.

1. Cut a piece of tracing paper slightly larger than the handkerchief. Trace one or more of the suggested motifs onto it until you have covered the same area as the handkerchief. You can use any combination of motifs to make your own paisley design.

2. With the fabric crayons, outline and color in your design on the tracing paper.

3. Iron the handkerchief flat. Reverse the tracing paper so that the design is face down, and place it on top of the handkerchief.

4. Iron over the tracing paper to transfer the design to the handkerchief. (Always ask an adult to help you iron.)

The Pacific

The Pacific is the region that includes Australia, New Zealand, and thousands of different islands in the South Pacific Ocean. People lived on some of the islands for thousands of years without contact with the outside world. As a result, they developed their own languages, customs, and traditional clothes without the influences of other cultures. For example, more than 700 different languages are spoken on the islands of Papua New Guinea, and many different styles of traditional costume have developed.

As in other parts of the world, people use the natural materials in their area to make traditional clothing. On the islands of the Pacific, these include seeds, leaves, grasses, tree bark, shells, fur, feathers, and sea creatures.

In the highlands of Papua ▶ New Guinea, bush people wear very little clothing. But elaborate headdresses and collars made of many natural materials are worn at traditional ceremonies.

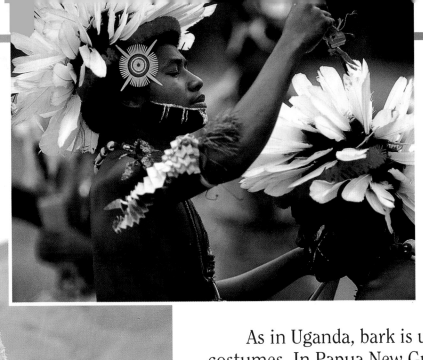

◀ The feathers and plumes of birds are an important part of many Pacific costumes.

Main picture: Barkcloth, called tapa, has been used to make this rain cape. The skirt is made of dried grasses.

As in Uganda, bark is used to make traditional costumes. In Papua New Guinea and the Pacific Islands, the inner bark of a mulberry tree is beaten, dried, and decorated. This bark, called tapa, is used to make a wraparound garment worn by women, and also a kind of apron, called a *malu*, worn by men. For this, the bark is made into a narrow strip of fabric that hangs down from the waist. *Malu* are also made of dried grasses or woven material.

Among some of the highland peoples of Papua New Guinea there are important ceremonial pig hunts, which are followed by huge feasts. These festivals are a way of keeping traditional beliefs alive. Each group exchanges pigs and shells, and elaborate costumes are worn to show off the wearer's wealth and importance. Part of these costumes, especially for male dancers, includes leg and arm decorations made of clay, wood, shells, and fur.

The feathers of birds are a favorite decoration for fancy headdresses in this part of the world. The Mekeo men, who live on the Papuan coast, wear huge headdresses made from the colorful feathers of the bird of paradise. The headdress of each village group has its own design, involving a complicated mixture of wood and feathers. In the Trobriand islands, traditional male dancers wear costumes made of the feathers of white cockatoos and black cassowary birds.

Today, some of these traditional costumes are made using modern sewing machines, instead of being made by hand. The materials included in the clothes of the Pacific region sometimes reflect more outside influences. An example of this is a traditional grass skirt decorated with the labels from old cans. The grass skirts is a well-known type of traditional dress. On the Solomon Islands and in Samoa, grass skirts are made of strips of banana leaves and dried in the sun. Then they are bound together on a waistband. Some parts of the skirt are dyed to produce multicolored stripes.

Another kind of traditional grass skirt is found in the Pacific island of Hawaii. This is part of the costume of the traditional hula dancers. Performers wear skirts made from green ti leaves, decorated bodices, and flower garlands called leis. A more modern tradition, both for men who live in Hawaii and often for visitors, is to wear an aloha shirt. These are brightly colored, short-sleeved shirts decorated with motifs such as parrots and palm trees. The shirts are so famous that they are known around the world as "Hawaiian shirts."

Both Australia and New Zealand were inhabited for thousands of years before European settlers started to move there two hundred years ago. In New Zealand descendents of the original Maori people, like the Australian Aborigines, normally wear modern clothing. However, they are eager to keep their old traditions alive and wear special costumes to perform Maori dances. The costumes are

made of a woven flax called *taniko*. This is dyed black, yellow, or reddish-brown and is used to make a traditional skirt called a *piupi* that is worn by both men and women. In Australia, the Aboriginal peoples have few traditional costumes, but instead decorate their bodies with paint for special occasions.

People from many different countries settled in Australia, and the descendants of those settlers still feel a link with their various countries. Some

◀ These Maori men are wearing traditional costumes to perform a ceremonial war dance called a *haka*. Such dances are part of the Maori's ancient customs, known as *Maoritanga*.

▲ These traditional Maori skirts, or *piupi*, would once have been worn on their own. But today's young Maori girls wear western-style shorts underneath.

of them have national costumes, which they wear on traditional days. There is an area in the Barossa Valley in South Australia that was settled by a group of German immigrants. One of Australia's most popular wine festivals is held in this region, during which folk dancers wearing traditional leather breeches called *lederhosen* can be seen celebrating German traditions. In the city of Sydney, Greek women dancers wear colorful boleros, aprons, and scarves to perform Greek dances during the special festivals. As in other parts of the world, costumes from many cultures can be seen in Australia today.

Although most of us wear modern clothes, traditional costumes have a special place in our world. They keep alive the memory of the world in which our ancestors lived. Wearing traditional costumes brings the past and present together in a beautiful way.

45

Glossary

Ancestors – One's relatives from the distant past.

Appliqué A type of embroidery using one or more layers of material.

Boleros Very short, tight-fitting jackets.

Breeches Half-length trousers gathered in at the knee.

Cassowary A New Guinea bird related to the emu.

Clan A family group.

Cummerbund A wide sash worn around the waist.

Fibers Fine strands from a plant or animal that can be made into a textile.

Flounces Frilly strips of material sewn to a dress.

Folk Originating from, or traditional to, the people of one country or area.

Geometric Consisting of groups of simple shapes, points, and lines.

Hide Animal skin.

Lent The forty days before Easter, when Christians fast or give up something important in memory of Jesus Christ.

Looms Tools used to weave cloth.

Manufacture To make something, often in a factory.

Mass-produce To make a large number of goods using machines.

Merino A breed of sheep.

Middle East The area around the East Mediterranean, especially Israel and the Arab countries.

Migrate To move with other people to live in a different part of the world.

Moccasins Soft leather shoes without a heel, originally worn by Native Americans.

Motif A repeated shape or picture used as decoration.

National costume The traditional clothes of a country.

Nomadic Moving from place to place to find food and land.

Persecution Ill-treatment of people, often because of their religious or political beliefs.

Poncho A triangular or circular cloak with a hole in the middle for the head.

Symbol Something that stands for something else.

Tanned Soaked in a vegetable or mineral solution.

Textiles Fabric or cloth, especially woven cloth.

Turban A head-covering formed from a long, winding piece of material.

Books to read

Baker, Wendy. *Fashion.* Hands-On. New York: Thomson Learning, 1994.

Lancaster, John. *Fabric Art.* Fresh Start. New York: Franklin Watts, 1991.

Rosen, Mike. *Summer Festivals.* Seasonal Festivals. New York: Bookwright Press, 1991.

Rowland-Warne, L. *Costume.* New York: Alfred A. Knopf Books for Young Readers, 1992.

Whyman, Kathryn. *Textiles.* Resources Today. New York: Gloucester Press, 1988.

Information about individual cultures may also be found in the 48-volume Cultures of the World series by Marshall Cavendish Corporation (North Bellmore, NY), or in your library's encyclopedia.

Index

The costumes in this book come from many different peoples. Various types of costumes are listed in the index, for example "hats," "dresses," and "scarves." If you want to see how costumes are used, look at entries such as "ceremonies," "dance," and "festivals." You can use the "peoples" entry to look up costumes from the cultures mentioned in the book. If you are making a costume and you need some ideas, look at the "decoration," "design," "materials," and "motifs" sections.